T0348660

I Woke a Lake

The Mountain West Poetry Series

Stephanie G'Schwind, Donald Revell, Kazim Ali,
Dan Beachy-Quick & Camille T. Dungy
series editors

We Are Starved, by Joshua Kryah
The City She Was, by Carmen Giménez Smith
Upper Level Disturbances, by Kevin Goodan
The Two Standards, by Heather Winterer
Blue Heron, by Elizabeth Robinson
Hungry Moon, by Henrietta Goodman
The Logan Notebooks, by Rebecca Lindenberg
Songs, by Derek Henderson
The Verging Cities, by Natalie Scenters-Zapico
A Lamp Brighter than Foxfire, by Andrew S. Nicholson
House of Sugar, House of Stone, by Emily Pérez
&luckier, by Christopher J Johnson
Escape Velocity, by Bonnie Arning
We Remain Traditional, by Sylvia Chan
The Lapidary's Nosegay, by Lara Candland
Furthest Ecology, by Adam Fagin
The Minuses, by Jami Macarty
Dears, Beloveds, by Kevin Phan
West : Fire : Archive, by Iris Jamahl Dunkle
Daughters of Harriet, by Cynthia Parker-Ohene
Susto, by Tommy Archuleta
A Face Out of Clay, by Brent Ameneyro
I Woke a Lake, by Susan McCabe

I Woke a Lake

POEMS

SUSAN McCABE

The Center for Literary Publishing
Colorado State University

For information about permission to reproduce
selections from this book, write to
Permissions
The Center for Literary Publishing
9105 Campus Delivery
Colorado State University
Fort Collins, Colorado 80523-9105.

Printed in the United States of America.

Library of Congress Cataloging-in-Publication Data

Names: McCabe, Susan, 1960- author.
Title: I woke a lake : poems / Susan McCabe.
Other titles: I woke a lake (Compilation)
Description: Fort Collins, Colorado : The Center for Literary
    Publishing/Colorado State University, 2025. | Series: The Mountain/West
    Poetry Series
Identifiers: LCCN 2025001735 (print) | LCCN 2025001736 (ebook) | ISBN
    9781885635938 (paperback) | ISBN 9781885635945 (ebook)
Subjects: LCGFT: Poetry.
Classification: LCC PS3613.C324 I33 2025 (print) | LCC PS3613.C324
    (ebook) | DDC 811/.54--dc23/eng/20250207
LC record available at https://lccn.loc.gov/2025001735
LC ebook record available at https://lccn.loc.gov/2025001736

The paper used in this book meets the minimum requirements of
ANSI/NISO Z39.48-1992 (Permanence of Paper).

To Anna Maria Martinson

And for Kate—and our life at Entrada for twenty-five years

Contents

I Woke a Lake

Tasting the Last of the Ice Age

We stuffed our mouths with snow
& bark on sleds to the border.
The ice hotel was not forgot.
Sleds kept their ice caps on
& skidded between forest folk~
they waved, they cried, we saw it all.

We live in the hotel beyond estrangement.

It floods sinks swerves—
Ultraviolet auroras on postcards slip
from raining frames.
The diamond chandeliers
hold prismatic sleepers
between glass sheets.
When staircases come down
we lose distinctions.
Still thrilled, yes, thrilling as ever—
the midnight sun stays on & on.

We do not anyway think of leaving.
Cities nearly all torched.
Pull-apart bodies stagger
into melting ice. One
drinks from a frozen glass
then drinks the glass too,
face at frost removes.
Flakes ache to re-constellate.

This dawn a pair of lovers,
were trapped in an ice alcove, caving,
beneath a smeared Patagonia
cover & puffer jacket on p. 53.

Stone told—"look under me."
They were already dead.
Hardly anyone notices a tender
chilling bliss. The giant cumuli
are walk-ons for permanence.
All the slow night they are there.

I Take Off the Suit of Never Mind

Just came out of a fire, just in
from another, rare are the proximity suits.
Weep holes don't hold. Water in all our days.

Let a tsunami crash against my
wet suit. Let the tides call for higher
hemlines, tipped glasses,
ebb stemmed.

In a V-neck draped with stiff lilacs
let me simmer under a frosty half-moon,
before brief farewell—or
I'll wear the bougainvillea
though branches cut.

A drop of blood here & there
part of the pattern.
I prepare to be a bit dissected.

Just washed in on another riptide with
bleached coral bits
& plasticine stuck to skin,
with seaweed bulb earrings.

I only wanted a moon-basking stream
to run a cool hand under its lovely,
without the clasp of oil-stuck sand.

Else we robe ourselves in apathy.
Look! There slinks ghost fur,
so many thinned & thirsty, while
others burn in distressed jeans.

Your pool is a dark brooch.
Don't go in, darling, it's too small.

Better wear the thick mustard sleaves
of spoiled air. Better to know you are
summoned, now, everywhere.

Tjikko

All lakes belong to me,
though not Lake Leman.
All lakes in poems belong to me.
Just let the laughter run over me.
I just let it, come I say, & it comes.
I own nothing. My shadow ripples
across lakes. *Solaces are mine*.
Once. All trees are mine. All
roots, the clean air, the molecules
of carbon & oxygen mine.
I am at the foot of a sooty
trench leading to a shut
mine. My great-uncle
worked in copper,
the red paint striking
all the houses. The
sulphur is mine. It is in my
lip gloss. I am a girl
watching in my mind's eye
this uncle taken to an asylum.
He grieved a class-crossed love.
A kick to his skull took him.
His mine was mine.

The maple in my mother's yard
held fast on the road Trotzgatan,
distal to the church in
the center of town. The late dog
is mine. I let laughter run over
me. No one is lost with such a spire,
or tree. Mine are the Dalecarlian horses,
their yellow & blue harnesses.

Mine my grandmother's accordion,
doubling for lungs, heaving blood.
Mine her hidden in the branches.
From the thirteenth century,
heaps carried up toward the light
of evening & laid on sheets.
One preserved in salts,
propped against the church.
His widow faints at the sight
decades after he is gone,
the ringing river glinting.

Small Park in the Lake

In a past the child props on elbows beside a
fading lake, clouds visible, half of a bridge

in reflection. She's still here, treading the banks.
In this overexposed, aging photo of her

she smiles, missing teeth, elbows
holding up for her brother's shutter.

The grass slopes to the small lake
at Cloverfield Park.

Bamboo stirs water, profiles of bounceable
ducks, dunking under for food bits—

how long will her face last?

Light erases light. A trail opens
on the still, plump banks.

A Woman Whose Larynx Hummed Yellow
for Cat

The living room lamps have golden shades.
Light adjusts rightly as throat warmth, well beyond
being handsome handmaid.
Library books record changing colors
of the high stained glass windows of Doheny.
What bubbles, continuous umlauts loving
shade & borders December over defined.
My mouth opens slightly.

Yes, this is a charmed valiant night, color of
the word heart. Wherever I stood in this small house
I could extend it. The window even
hums open with tulip birds when
an umlaut crowns over.

My mouth swallows, the larynx a well
deep as any redbreast.
Umlauts lap in the birdbath
under the window's ledge,
the kitchen rectangularly pregnant.

I splash beyond dishes, splashing
screens, granite, hands.
(Cat said *wash dishes like smoking
a joint, you can just drift.*)

A sudden cry:
There's an umlaut in my umlaut. After
all, Roman numerals undid the empire.

Afloat, I lie down on tinted lawns,
etched. Night hoods an outdoor theater,

about to collect the sky's chatter—yes
I beat against its chest, spilling
over—& line up votive candles
to flicker in cerulean glass.

There will be blue eggs tomorrow.
No omelets or mixed vegetables, no eyelashes.
There's only one lake in the word umlaut
though it sounds like many swilling
the quiet evening, the mind easing to set off,
like the lamps with colors passing through
votives. The lamps wait for
forgetful anticipation of habitat.

Heads bow, bathing in several tints.
Umlauts keep rising.

I had a brackish shade from Florence once. I eat biscuits,
gulp effervescent darkness at the back
of the throat like coffee grounds
that scale cherry tree mountains, hang
umlauts dotting spines of succulents.
The yellow roses never bloomed, never died—

I trail my fingers in a wave cresting miles away,
& with my mind travel from my house
down the mountain to the hinted shore or
to the library full of humming.
One long textured breath,
a sudden vowel, leaning behind
a front balcony of iris & pond.
Two circles rise, stereoscopic islands

at the shores of twin lamps.
Exhalation is now complete.

This way I can follow where I am going,
where I want to go. I think I know
where I am going.

I Woke a Lake

I.

numberless bones mumbling,   coughing & feeding, clouded
glaucous eye, living downward where

it's not Grasmere & no bells exalt me,   instead hysteresis
              I am not anywhere I know

watercress protected by rough shale, gashed, & loaming, loamed, in
              the littoral zone & mists, fumes, tadpoles, slim fish.

Remember the leech gatherer, stooped over shriveled ponds,
              coal-spoiled—
                        a train bends
distance,
                        his matted coat receding within winds:

Sail this perimeter,   yet first find it!

2.

A paragraph loves longer wave-swells   my love is to open,
          never a container,   rather luminous wet, chills
                    heaving wavelets , blurred.
I mime muteness   freedom from inevitability.

Picnickers   with puff vests, sticks in a basket,
                    one seeking unseen birds.
Then it was time to pack up the picnic
clouds;
                    trash sweeps toward raveling edges—

I must keep my subtle ceiling up, my forest-
          mind, moving
across a blind valve & copper stark night, for

this vastness   gives sometimes   impossible
                              restlessness,
          never making it around,
                              a proximate practice

3.

In stillness-making, I am a force that
condenses, combines
        say, a perfume hatbox or mascara boots
                of a wanderer's macrobiotic notebook tips
into my dilating imperfection.
        I'm not anywhere I don't know.

A human lay briefly in liquid shadow.

In water, shape never stays, giddiness stirring, especially here
        an ever-shifting mud chalice   reaching for elsewhere sisters,
clay clutches lying in heaps,   yet bubbles rise up
        always from shadow   this spot for the least of birds
not prisoners of the bark!

                        I dreamed a carriage ponied around, never
sensing my multi-bodied aluminum, scrub nettle; glowworms,
        lit yellow veins
                corn gold in mirror; ferns spreading
                keep my shirt glass up still.

Sometimes bodies just fall through   ~relatives~
        sediment with loose bits
            & doubtful substance

4.

I never search carefully never very
Loving lying down on myself
      like a lens, &   touching shore grass recently
          trembled me

An eternal someone checks soot levels, alkaline, mulch, fowl,
      a blanket temporarily pulled across an eyelid.

          There's a quiet maenadic murmur here, seeking

other rivulets,   distant throbbing relatives,
mixed with
lead gray, yellow leakage.

This lake gives hallucinations. This, my quarry, my smrd txt,
    trying not to quake so near the once-active mine
        churning   red paint   for wooden cottages
& for singing bowls   quartz & meteorite-made iron

. . . I
remain collected   smoothing out, really to photo-
synthesize purple loosestrife, water milfoil,   labor worth it

for who can defy me—synthesizer of grand fugue evenings with
enormous contact with other bodies, my aural fate

& men disappear
      leading to inverse stratification—
          loose granules, rifts—brandy picnics

5.

I wake up an excitable rim,
        bursting lilac, lilacs
                Here, after the storm, the picnic rustled

After trout just slipped in &   all endured cheerfully
Among four-legged ghosts, fiddle ferns, gully ingle gossip:
I
luxuriate   in my own   elixir
both center & edge wobble, being

born from a meteor,   that cratered
        150,050 miles wide, 3,050 feet
                deep   377 million years ago:

my ring is   porous rock   magnets   altering air into
        laughing gas

sending messages to Tjikko, the 9,550-year-old Norway Spruce
        in a trance~   thin   verdant as ever,   it
endures
its roots holding under moss & snow   reaching out

        to   sisters in   daubs of blue-clouded time

6.

Send radio waves to skim water,

    after all, I lie

out as I do, shining where

        . . . I can, distributing . . .

7.

Hope enjambs with search
only to smash into circumference ,

a Falcon '58   still warm   at my bottom
caught it breathing   in my largesse,
not moody just pure mood !

Pummel canoe, skiff, corpse trees from last storm,
        try to defy me &
                I don't know where I am not

I love smoothing out, hover is my way ,
        After all, I am always more than I am
                at the end of , , , , tunnel , , , , of the mind

Eleusinian

I have stood talking to the corn behind a wood fence.

My psyche relies on mycelium.
     Chanterelles, porcinis, morels
     burst in my daughter's mouth.

*

During the first days below
     I did count & break small seeds, little sacs

around them, my mouth
pushing back integument after integument restraining
     my longing for return:
     an eternal pastime of
     all too soon?

You are reception writ in
     shimmering fungal strands, hair
     burgundy one sees by way of bubbles.

Are we in the sea yet?

Or do we just spiral up & down at will
to touch the shrine's navel, or lie
on trembling waters,
where ornaments of grain, mostly dead, wash up?
I am fed up with the cult of ugliness,
     a pounding terrible of
     uncertain butterflies, soaring across lupine.

The yellow months sent news
of what might survive yet. Even
      you know limits.

In each other's magnetic hold we speak
      with no device except ether.

I do but need more candles, &
      those caps you set float on
      the surface of your broth.

Orchard

There's a fruit tree in my brain,
      in the blurred distance:
      an orchard, its fruit trees, outside time,
      waiting for that second of ripening.
      Orchards once did grow here. Inland empire
blindly cut them, for its many boxes,
      on old ground, de-nurtured.
      Let some rainy fragrance make it through
veils—   Orchards O!
      & those that grew in sea kettles.
      How we gasped,
      picking those fallen, then climbing,
      their thick skin some protection.
      Not quite what the swaddling hibiscus
      does for itself. It dies intact,
ready for a journey.

I see two students, girl-lovers hand in hand.
      A friend booms—"hey
      you lovebirds"—this a shock after months of contagion.
—here a little careless spark ignites chards . . .
      By now a perfectly formed tree grows in my brain
      with those sweet lemon orange plum & tangerine.
      Crates full. I'm a hummingbird feasting on September,
purring for sugar from sun leaf & flower . . .

Stars, be safe from satellites clawing you from our
hair, like flowers that only open just before twilight—

There are orchards in my brain's trunk,
      rooting the optic stalk, buried rail tracks, a city
      reaching east from ghost cornfields where

children toss limes in bright light though
the highest apple is never found. This orchard
starts in the corpus collosum: The seeds ripen

while stray birds light a match, red heads
running across a strip, & every word crackles

to flower. Ripe is usually ripe enough. Tasting
love-breath is not too dangerous, & wavelengths
travel from crown to perineum, the mind grows everywhere.

Yellow swarms enter between seconds. Yet
a weekend on the road flees fire. Weekenders
flee fire in electric motors. Such burnt fleece almost normal here.

Dread never ceases when ladling Hesperides—
how many bowls left?

Nothing resembles a human face as much as
wet mold pigmented with fruit features. There are
misplaced crates, hives—there's an active impulse
toward decay—

so come cloud, come
grass blades, cut me an ancient rose . . .

Tarim Princess

You are nearly
four millennia old.
You are so stylish, wearing
a pointy, white felt cap,
& twigs as stay buttons.
Your hair is bulky straw.

You went in a dry boat
through the Bronze Age that always
has longing sea breezes
        in it, un-wrinkling folds of statues.
There is water around you before
you die. Inert & still. Eventually,
the desert salt kept you dry, enough powder
for your high cheekbones.

Later you walk streets beside Baudelaire unaware
you are a true haunt. Who had women lovers.
Your eyes deeply pocketed, perfect lashes,
        almost you glide above pavements
with your fur-lined boots.

        Herb ephedra in your basket,
wrapped in cowhide,
your plaid garment melds with
bone, ribs, scapula.

You are almost intact.

Dead I've Spoken to Lately

are quite happy to be dead
It isn't that they know
everything but that they're
occupied with listening

They know we don't want
to hear them or see them really
We call out when we come home

They are content
(Even our animals say it's fine)

They are busy in deflected brightness
They can be awry, not unhappy. Giving up
on us would not be the same. They can
be present. Our cornflower faces
dip in ink—

These dead are busy between points
They are sorry they can't
help it

Their time is concentric
Flowers please them
Goldenrod dust & beaten
daisies in cones of dirty water

They especially like water changing colors
It isn't completely easy, it can't
be entirely learned how *not* to seek out the
dim lights

They wish you'd move this book
you're reading so the page could be discerned

Apparitional

Remember to wear the goggles for this one.
Or it might throw you to the uneven floor.
Its flesh flows through a cellular nightgown.

I don't see her walking. But she must
for she deposits in my open palm a little
dirt & roots—she holds my face

for a moment, held as
if not part of a skeleton.

Remember to polish the back brain's lens,
make a scaffold of leaf and vine.

It was full sun when I saw
'Annah, in Harrari cape.
"You are my star," she said,

as she stood in the air.
I had a long walk through inter-

locking forests of Berlin.
Cal was staying at a hotel
where he slept slim on a cot

jammed against other cots.
I wanted to wake him

to drive me to another hotel.
But the camping class would begin.
Two women gave me a puff
& wanted me to stay

in the forest café!!

Don't forget your
ice boots for undulant waters.

Ready yourself. Call &
the cure usually comes.

Uphill

We peer into our phones as
occult prayer books, or cradle
them like dear faces.
The phone man Dylan said
they are limbs we grow.
      Named after Dylan Thomas, he was doomed
to drink & poetry, he said, now in recovery,
finding spark in chasms
—He did a deep reset &
sent us on our ways into ample arms

of summer. The poppies like going on but
      a bell rings thrice & still sticks like burrs.
You only stream once someone says. Now there are
      real clouds! Mist fizzes! Rising into the palisades—
Love what is left   affection grows out & in.
Burnt pampas sways,

a sparrow obsessive pecks a dirt mound for seeds
then hits its cranium at the stone wall,
obsessional. Phones obsolesce.
Some won't respond to touch. A friend said "fading,"
I heard "fating." Prayer books

grow bacteria in libraries. Vine flowers call
hummingbirds, who stop midair in front
of my garden chair.

Now a white-haired man on roller-
blades pummels up Entrada, his portable radio
playing "Landslide," the words
"took my love, took it down"
fading uphill.

When in Love Goes Fear

I am a boudoir full of crushed roses.
I never did get to finish my story about the Baltic.
The cold waves slapped the heavens.
We walked the pier, we spoke of cables,
their odd receptivity to our vocables. In the water
my body could not be seen. Rain cut
into the sea with diamonds. My legs came up
for breath. I swam around the lightning,
not toward the messenger.

I went ahead of my vision—as usual
at the end of the pier before my body
had lengthened the way
the ocean was already swallowed—
a tongue of sight pulled back into throat, &
most of the boats were swallowed—the
past tense had caught up with me.

When in love goes fear of lack of others
almost at the curving horizon.
Then to turn back, admitting failure
to encompass the day's slightly less familiar
eucalyptus & palms, walked by a million times,
in another climate not the Baltic's, but standing before
the wide Pacific, now to be a morsel
while my speech soared on above the pines,
barely touched by the lifting lithium air

—Sometimes I stop to stare at bark & skin
in leaves with messages folded in,
to touch & to see at once was not my allowance,

yet not to touch & still to see
was worse! There's no sake, for anyone,
like the present rain: no presenter,
no pleasanter raincoat for how my mind
is near thunderclouds, yet never in them.

A voodoo second that was gone before
sighted—they were there in the whorls
of waves when I missed the tall & lanky
bearded messenger who lapped away.
Was it he who looked like her?
The ice cream vendor was no longer there.

It was nearly winter, but not to be
forgotten was the icy summer in
the dark of money, deep dives.
There were scores, more than scores of
these fledglings: trickery in grass,
concrete hair, hair of dirt left alone—
No money was as costly as a past
like an iron negligee thrown down.

Her thighs (was she the messenger?)
were red & gold by turns, her scalp beneath
her hair uneven, she felt the down growing up
in the elevator, with the sea still in sight,
to find the spine, a chord where
mystery lies. I bring my digital lamp
for I'm now communicating like crazy:
units in procession, for a fleece of
motion & energy—

A brain is lighter than a personality,
more compact. (Those people I met on the Baltic
shore, they married & divorced *as* personalities;
they met that way & never unmet.
They were never never like us.)
Standing on the wobbling pier,
we were soft foam of Vienna, more, even aura,
a halo that was inside, also outside.
Did I finish my story about the Baltic?
Large ice cubes in our arms,
glaciers under glass, specimens to someone's
undersea camera: we never wore suits! You were
there, but I will tell you what it was like.

I had been treating one of
my lungs. Patients would confuse
other patients for doctors, one almost
leapt or flew from a ledge.
I talked her down, tide up & a silver line
cut the ocean, darkness from darkness.

The verbose waves of this Baltic were closer
than I had thought, in my dreams.
Then I was *in* the Baltic, its waves thicker,
more unknown than the familiar slaps
of the Pacific. I do plan to finish
my story on the Baltic.
Our glasses begged for whiskey
though it was summer.
The suspicious one
I almost recognized had left his sauna.

He left in his smart car, shook off his carapace.
He had backache & left with such secrets!
Without a word in print is to go off the edge—
I stayed in the ice hotel with chill face &

remember the pool of minerals,
that misted up our faces, especially yours,
whose I was always, it seemed, looking
for. You were lost every second or so.
Dipped in or out of vision. You greeted
me wearing a layered parka—I practically tore the fur
out looking for a message.
"All my codes should not
be understood," you said.
Half your face was blurred, the other
half not, like I could see you dreaming . . .
I walked toward you
along filigreed rails. Told to keep our distance:
I still saw your sheets of lace.

Agents are usually invisible, or in halftones,
part in and part out of focus.
We can have all sorts of invisibles, even
angels. I see them every day when waves crash
while midnight ropes me from the bottom
of my glass. Ice to ice, homeopathic.

Here's one, I said, that must take on
some humble reality, a person not a personality,
residue of a full sun at night when we
were frozen away from feeling:

One who'd walk the earth & cut her or his hair
tomorrow as today, storing the Baltic as memory:
the place where you, for once, dropped artifice
& gave in to luxuries of drowning
& then discovered the thrill of

—the air!   Watch out, for it picks up everything.

Catalogue I

Because I furiously try to control things
       the braille of turreted altocumulus in pink outside my
control, like the spikes of the revived faux gothic that can't

help from sprouting the campus a new wing, with rational
perspective. I'm helpless before such gradual sudden change.

Suddenly, I appear frozen—but new things
eat & pick over old ones. Some of the stranger lights up,
springs showing. I can't control my sister's obsessions, nor

my own. Nor what happened to my father or my older
half brother, both alcoholics. My mother's pain remained
underground. I spied the fates unthreading.

No one could control the drinking. Not the army. Not his
schoolmarm sisters, & I can't control climate disasters,
       the orphan population, save the abused animals.

I send money to *Save the Children, World Wildlife Fund, Save the Redwoods,*
Amnesty International. I can't
control my thought waves so I make cloud gestures,

send them along in worry boats that bear down fast
send gusts I cannot control to buoy them along.

The braiding stream's fabric, wavelet by wavelet, tiny
boat by tiny boat, tendered to some place where they slide
from form. So easy
when they drift in the periplum. When I am
trapped in the discursive, I imagine what it might be like
to let my air trine lift me up
       from materiality's enduring claim

into awareness without a mirror, above the echoes
that corner the ears, the caves knowing just this:

You can't handle ancient beasts, or
slay some necessary gritted sadness that seeps
into a time that flows & stops as well.

Let all harms, crimes, chimeras—capsize!

Sappho in Recovery

Loving & liking so much & then, this quick gasp. I am not someone who likes
to wound. Hooked to self-help books. *Dancing as fast as I can,* and now all
of Pema, *living how we will die.* Say horizon is impossible. *I have a quiet mind.*
Show your safe crackers anyhow. We did the double cross, the triple cartwheel
in air. In the quietest chamber in us. Come here, while your lover brushes
away hurt tangles, dear. You watch your faun's hair swinging across a bare
torso. Doorstep, lintel, sill. Muses have dropped gold. No one can give me
my green back but my green field. The sky white as an egg. How the spruces
shake my mind, wind rushing through. They draw up a clear brave water. Your
books, shelved in old light, readiness for a sail. I want to dissolve on call—in
bed last night I was—billowing—trace lines across space. It couldn't last. In
the open form of my love, my stomata gulps the soft air. Still, hair sticks to my
mouth, & I speak when I should not. Manned boats set off, & none delivers
you~~~

They Moved Whole Forests, While I Slept

When they cut them from the ground
l was dumb, & not dumb.
Heavy steel trucks lumbered & raced
      through the small northern
      town in my nightmares—

where l once lived, teaching in the Forest.
Ah Eugene! Willamette Valley, river ill.
      Trucks barreled highways,
      their steel bolted corpses.

l recognize nothing here anymore.
      Only
High Street where you can still
buy a jar of coffee beer to go.

Tree stumps in a hotel act as
      memorial side
tables, leftover ancientness
to offer casual fruit; a plaque on each
amputee memorializes that such &
such a tree lived
here & here & here.

War. The Exile and the Rock Limpet.
after a painting by Turner

More teeth than the slipper snail, the limpet clings
to its rock. The nearby river is shrinking
with molten blue possibility, volcanic ash & rain.
At Helena, home means hallucinogenic sails.
Napoleon wears his uniform, inspecting the sand,
its affinity with emperor-solitude, with fixity.

He spies a limpet, a gastropod, patella vulgata,
conical, less coiled than most snails, sprinkled with
cinnabar white to diffuse poisonous yellow,
a color that attracts . . .
Is this to be your land, Ostend, of mossy caverns,
with gaseous forgetfulness?
He thought the gastropod beckoned when
it indicated limp away:

patella holding the island, cut with vermillion
rocks, rapidly losing any solidity.
Rock teeth suck in red light to unfurl
a last robe.

A Letter to Another Poet on Rilke & Fusion

The mirror has its own room, too. Consider.
There is another side to the body's story . . .
Especially after I felt your love poems late last
night vibrate & then
heard the yelling of a couple, those who
long warred above, the wife,
in a red sweater at bay window,
in that hilltop villa. The fiery voices
of dogs need to speak . . .
The hill heaves boulders to us below after
the latest storms.

The owl on a persimmon branch has fourteen
vertebrae while we have only seven.
I can only try to see behind me.
Both my beloved and I have sight issues.
Both of us have a hobble, now & then.

We learn today of a discovery
to liberate us from nuclear energy. Trade
atoms for making fluid by heat. *Fusion*.
My wife visualized it
as two pregnant women coming into contact . . .
to form one & somehow the process
leaves leftover abundance,
meringue clouds, electrical love . . .

The future enters into us, says Rilke.
I am glad to meet his angels in your poems,
and yes—he did
have intimacy problems.

He was constitutionally unfit,
flying with one suitcase on his hunt for an
enormous unseen hum.
Did he fail by falling for eternity?
Decade after decade, country to country,
castle to castle, his angels came as he sought
the mineral in the mountain that turns crystal . . .

At last, a long row of outstretching junipers
offers a long drive.
All shouts recede while I walk,
the daily argument on the hill, the bark of
a bullhorn directing kids to dance
dwindles. I trust my senses, & my feet
as I am unsure which side of the mirror
to step in: Rilke says we must live both sides.

Insatiable, I seal my mineral extract: for
all's useless, without a crucial
expanding, *taking in.*
I thought *I* lived under a cliff,
pulling up herbs, but I see the anemone
sleeps wide open, facing it all.

Brasserie

Hybrid club: only part or min.
one drop human, only granted in.
Waiters dress & behave humanly.

Entrance: a glass case of eyeless
polar bears in festive colors,
ancient oddments, rings, a

pudgy jeweled aristocrat framed:
all favor this activity of devouring,
things fadged to look like something else.

Foie gras (frau gross, spell-check corrects)
passed a test to be on the menu. The divorced
husband, with his soft-eyed son (a socialist),

his hair dangles across an uncertain future,
his Tesla juiced & waiting, & his sister
has an eyeless bear from a butterscotch wheel.
           Where did their love go.

Toothpicks walk away someday. What pain
you swallow must you bear. Father didn't want
his daughter crying. Wrack of guilt, winged veal.

State of Emergency when we force-feed
ducks to swell livers. Gavaged, can't even stand.
Shrimp prop in a cocktail by blood ampules.

It's for kids, a vampiric ideal, when sunrays
hit mid-robotic. Monsanto plus Polymorphic,
(not in a good way . . .)

Pain, turns out, can be served à la carte.
Lead Belly on low . . .

Rib pulled, replanted. Rib wriggles, danced like
Rita Hayworth on the plate, everything starts up,
trying to look or moan like something else.

Humans cyborg their plates:
Have you tried the tatar? *My favorite by far.*
Quail eggs pop, so easy to do,

too-circular yolks, forked + stirred
to stick to thin vermicelli.
How about some tar tar tar tar tatar
bite-size (conforming to teeth); chicken rolls,
fish stick shaped, oh how buttery, swallow

down fast, the bird's muscle sinks.
What won't humans pay for
artifice on small plates. Dine family-style, food with

auto chips to speak between bites. What Psalm for this.
Isthmus ink in the lake. The broken home will be
isthmusing for Christmas on shores of Geneva.

Death is distinct from diet-death, or *Liquid Death©*:
still urchins eat the dregs,   we eat them.

On Coffee in Canada En Route to (and from) Elizabeth Bishop's Childhood Home in Great Village, Nova Scotia

How I read the sloped & hilled cups like Japanese
          prints, the delicacy of some future yet to be
How I sought my Deity Caffeine as I traveled
          town to town
How I planned to write a de Tocqueville in Canada
Because my first question when arriving in any town
is where is the really good coffee
for it is the latté everything depends upon
How the bubbles on the surface are the money of the pour
How Bach's Coffee Cantata felt like a thousand kisses
          after bowls of milky coffee
          I drank seriatim eight years before
on Garden Street, pursuing the mind's "proto-crypto"
          dream house
How the goats discovered the beans
          when they wandered from their shepherd &
          returned to the same tree the next day to frolic
How in Mahone Bay I waltzed in a 1860s house turned bookstore
          café & I played dominoes, ordered espresso after espresso
          to affirm my worldview, pricey with the Belgian chocolate
          with orange flakes
In the garden there you feel free
The Sufis used coffee to stay up all night but forgot the fazendas
I thought I should write a de Tocqueville in Canada
& how finding so few places of gathering dispirited
          yet here was the wild lilac air
Coveting a Joseph Cornell collage of percolator (cost: 60,000 dollars
          at the Antiquarian Book Fair), its glass knob so whimsical
          it brought back my mother's brew
How de Tocqueville would find much wrong even with bucolic
          highways and few billboards
(The great poem of addiction has been written
          & we know who wrote it)

De Toqueville did write about coffee as a source of all good
      ideas about democracy
      (we know this is & isn't true)
While Diderot & Franklin & Rousseau plotted revolution
      slaves labored with ideas as well as beans
How Starbucks has almost always had fair-trade coffee
      but only one shelf & I become lacrimonious
What if it could be a real way of life connecting us to the
      farmers & red clay ground & to
      berries in rain, to books we would write & read & discuss
Empires lift up on the backs of others
& the self just sits there & the junkie
      moves from place to place
We could choose to welcome the berries with more grace
      but this was meant to be something about addiction
When she started making it I started waiting for it
When I drank my twelfth cup I liked to think of Balzac
      making spacious novels
      "for the nightly labor begins and ends with torrents
      of this black water, as a battle opens and concludes
      with black powder"
& during the Civil War the South had only chicory & lived off slaves
      so lost the war & founded New Orleans
A man from Richmond fashioned a brooch
      with illustrious beans instead of diamonds
Did I say that when I planned my opus on coffeehouses in Canada
      those other things which for several reasons we won't mention
That a Just Us warehouse opened in Wolfville but closed the day
      I arrived after demonstrations about making coffee properly
      (+ the self in its water jar feeling filaments
      reach down & down)

La Comédie humaine grew in sixteen cups (2,600 miligrams?) daily on an empty
        stomach over a period of many years
& Beethoven ground precisely sixty beans to measure out
        his life to brew each cup
Did I mention I was going to write a self-help book
        on the "year of the rat" on how these creatures
        make their homes where they have to & that they are not abject
        & on how hard-work industry & will are all that matter
        (of this I was mistaken)
In Odd Books I bought a book by Wright & one by Hall & *Briggflatts*
        by Bunting & sat in Café Voltaire a bit weary
Did I say about the sinking
& how I wanted to buy every painting John Neville (local) painted
        near my dream house overlooking the bay
Because Bishop's childhood home in Great Village was a Grave
        Disappointment (still held her mother's scream
        in corners & across the bay from Halifax where the
        sanitarium echoed)
A Salem fire frightened mother & daughter & Bishop felt the
        "put that down" reprimand for touching ashy
        stockings in the aftermath
How I left the house after the first night even though I planned
        to stay a month, shipped boxes of books, &
        hollered by a creek after the house's broken
        machine left me stringing my clothes up to dry
        in motels across pining New Brunswick
At the Bay of Fundy pieces of fraying rope rolled in on waves
There was a cottage (not Bishop's) of many-colored stones that looked edible
& was well-swept plain & playful & had a sea view,
        a lasting dream & every rock glinted
Neville's paintings were of women pushing off in boats

where you couldn't tell the boat from the water, the water
from the boat, one woman sinking in like Ophelia among
the breathing plants & giving in to them
& how as I write you this poem coffee cools by my side

Catalogue II (An Incomplete Disaster Report)

Maui's gem capsized by winds
tearing down powerlines, & the ancient banyan
re-buds. Canada is still on fire,
& ashen Phoenix reached
record heat again, a hurricane is off Baja,
with a tropical storm headed for Los Angeles
A 5.5 earthquake went mostly unnoticed.
July was the hottest month
in all human history.
Fires blaze toward the tiptoeing Parthenon. July
is the hottest month.
It was like no other July, it doesn't matter
which one. Seabirds disappear from Norway's
cliffs. We are made
& unmade by atmosphere.

A fire rages beside a river in Ashland.
The Acropolis is on fire, as well as
nearby forests. This serious
weather we can hardly track—barely.

Let the emergency vehicles pass.
Let the scarlet hands of ivy crawl across
the wall, let the wall sway, let
wind reanimate the dying plants,
Let the emergency flashing ship pass
easily, worry boats in its wake.

In Los Angeles. 60,000 years ago
saber-toothed tigers, camels,
all manner of wild beasts, roamed:

we recover their bones
from the tar they left,
putting one bone
next to the other until more miles
are needed to reassemble these creatures
along Miracle Mile.
Before the last ice age, they
wandered freely in Los Angeles
enjoying stars,
treading high grasses, the rocky
crystal, waters immense.

When I ask students how they
rate their climate change anxiety
they waver between 5 & 6, not
too different from their rating of
Seasonal Affective Disorder.
They have withdrawn their hands.
They worry (mildly)
about future generations.
They think of all the colorful
windbreakers for wind coming in.

Now hurricanes & floods swallow Libya
the day before an earthquake
takes down pieces of Morocco . . . (this catalogue
only takes us through last October).

The terrible wars go on & on,

A Palestinian grows small vegetables
in broken tubs & basins.
Gaza
in ruins, unspeakable—

A famous poet dies,
A famous critic dies,

Footholds fall in.

        :

&
&
&

Channel

When I envy

      a girl who channeled a river,
        I remember it may have been me on a rusty-

green (French?) chair—I heard beware of sculpted stones

      that fall suddenly . . . from a failing slope.

Boulders didn't miss
      her rivering mouth last month.

        I try closing one eye to see

           a thirsty ghost cross-legged on sandbags in
             runnels of rain.

Too Deep to Disturb

I wake up early,
leash an invisible dog,
walk toward umbrellas:
petunia, pearl, green.
I think of those—who, centuries
ago, were mad with grasping,
trampling to plant these palms
back toward ocean postcards. In
the gardens, I study the paint on irises:
yellow streak, mild violet—
mad white. Jacaranda flowers empurple
pavements beside the Spanish houses.
I hear a colonizer's lusty echoes.
I dawdle. A surfer passes.
By the time I am home in
a mile, my hair is at least
twice as long as when I left.
Was my quiet too deep
for time to disturb?
I push the feast away

to say Yes.

An Abbreviated Queer Autobiography

Shirtless in shorts, I turned my face right
from the question, are you a girl—or a boy?
What did it matter, I was Christ,
words dissolved into that patch of sun on
radial dirt of our yard, mostly dirt.
Step into my light, I could have said.
Let me touch you, I might have said.
Shirtless, I angled my face . . .
pleasurable shame—like when
      the Girl Scouts turned me away, because
I was a boy, or
just some poor marginal thing
I stood there, took
a shower in reverse: waiting
for mud to thicken up to the lips.

*

I found time with my mother by eating candy,
having cavities,
selling candy at school.
I typed my own excuses.
The teacher sighed, "again."
I walked the plank across the nude room in my sister's
borrowed skirt. Mother knew I was a girl-boy
who loved adventure &
      had to have special education.

*

Standing up to brush my hair on a chair
I made two front strands
          & left my back hair as nest.
          Those who saw it tugged.
I still sold candy in the girl's room
          like Polka Gris-Britta, the nickname
          given my never-met grandmother of Falun,
who made cones of these striped candies for boys to sell.
I could
lose or trail behind
          my allowance at Rexall or spend it on candy, tiny
envelopes, a paperback of *The Stranger*
          because I liked the cover.

*

Years later, I met Madelaine becoming William. I didn't want her
bird-like breasts taped.

He liked when beggars called her "Sir."

Just exhausted by illegibility

& horror—

One swims in the margins . . .
I am one of the seven weepers.

To perform surgery on oneself
requires some anesthesia.

*

My mother, a performer, in drag before my birth,
toured with the USO.
It was natural to see my
      mother in costumes, as Johnny Ray,
      in plaid jacket, cigarette dangling from mouth, or as
      Marlene in black hat
      & tails, double cross-dressed, or as
      super femmes, singing through Betty Hutton.

I found my mother's makeup kit with dusted

Nembutal, scavenged from Mexico for her
      Viennese husband, a Jew, an older man, likely
queer, whose heart failed.

Mother saved the unused pills
      "in case" things got too bad.
      This is a real story with love in it.

At fifteen I tried a few of the pills to no effect.

*

They wanted a confession . . . I was ten.
      My mother, sister, and brother were there.
      Our foggy father died a year before.
They saw my perfect crime, so I couldn't be
      a kleptomaniac. Too calculated, too calculating,
I was wearing the evidence. I whispered to my mother

that I'd write the confession—only for them.

Santa Monica police, next to Sears with green deco lights,
hand-
cuffed, pale stringy one, finger-
printed, herded into a holding
cell (it had bars)
for what seemed a long while.

After my family soothed me with treats.
I slept through noon.
I sat on the log by our jungle
pampas, a muddy mound in sunlight
burning away sad edges.

Modern Family

Frozen, in custody, by the dozen,
egg-giver wants hers frozen

indefinitely; sperm-giver wants
them unfrozen _now_; he hunts

embryos in waiting for
a vessel, a mother or

a silver globe. He's found
a new mate, more sound.

A giant freezer holds
embryos in veils, & folds

labeled for security in
faded fog of kin,

a palazzo of trays
& care-counter-guy plays

loud music for this teeming
incipience—beaming,

he froze a dozen yesterday, fleet
with little feet,

headed toward an unknown
future, shrouded in down.

At work parties in the freezer,
candled-lab-nights, they drink teasers.

When the man comes in with *where
are they?* workers blankly stare.

He broke from a marriage bond
frantic to unfreeze a son.

My embryo, his ex-wife chants,
mine, indefinitely. You simply can't.

The x slips into the freezer
deeper than expected, his knees

on ice, he skids, a lab locker slides,
white smoke rolls over the tides

over numbers that can decay or
blur 8 into 0, or a 4

fades to 1 . . .

Nothing now can be done.

Recovery

The keys were behind the door. Temptation
was never the question. What was being said. The
door was open.
I wasn't surprised that my
       sunglasses were lost. If they had not gone

yesterday they would not have stared
up from the patio table.

Whenever I open the door
       I hide what is behind it.
          There they are. The lost keys behind the door.

I once bathed in a chemical chimera.

I had a friend who wanted to make a sculpture of
       all our empty drug bottles saved
       for smashing
       & glued together.
That art project was canceled due
       to a sudden death.

Why did I put the empties in the car?

Not to tempt, though they did,
but to materialize a new idea of an escape—

The Hungry House in Atherton

The trees are marching
toward the house and
those in it.
The trees are frozen

in arabesque.
The hungry house
incinerates whatever
comes too close or near—

the wild roses, the lettuce.
A plastic jellyfish cleans the pool.
Packages arrive with "GILT"
labels, picked up with haste:

those who live here
work through dawn past dusk
to feed a hunger
no orchard feeds.

This house un-haunted
can only eat, eat, eat:
it never gains in feeling,
never admits defeat.

Sturdy like the muskrat
or the cantilevered oak:
so radiant for itself it breathes.

The house spins & wastes with
more lettuce than it can share.
The sacks are packed
though never given.

Owners smell no rot.
They keep venture going,
unending rises in profit.
Gilt keeps arriving, arriving,

there's always a lot to eat
though somehow it withers
to the touch. The cottagers
who live along the edge

relax when the investors
leave, there now, a reprieve.

My wife picks up fallen plums
from the well-kept orchard.
Here plants devour
their own stems.

A code opens heavy gates.
Cottagers must park outside.
A grill drags down at night
over their glass door, snaps shut.

No moonlight can enter.

The Porsche lives beside
the pine-protected cottage.
Investment banker screeches,
revs, goes. Never a greeting

& no one ever breaks water in
the glistened pool the entire year.
Cottagers forbidden. *Oh, why,*

why are they here?
More packages arrive.
The belly still empty.
"We try for moderation,"
says banker's banker wife,

"Just back from an Alaskan cruise"
their stomachs were too full—
they prefer withers, shivers,
their hungry house even coos.

Elements of Earth, Hold On

All wander their own ways:
nitrogen + phosphorus + calcium + manganese, all at hand,

those hirsute pebbles, gather in a cocktail of
antidepressants, hormones, plastics.

All swing into zones unevenly marked like
wishes—for the dear earth of many-ness
& for sunbathing stones, their crumbling centuries.

Dead organisms tinier than grains possess
too little oxygen to decompose!!!!
There is a plan to sew extra invisible matter
to help them decompose a bit.

The epitome of the dead is oil—so
in burned Kern, its
mining accessories as tinfoil souvenirs.

Envisioning the earth's microorganisms from afar
stretches the mind's time sense to snap, without breath to
search soil's soul—.

These bones deplete calcium,
yet must—hold the figment of a person in place—
while rain tatters soil, loosing
the most tiny, vast earthlings.

Counting the Manuscripts

We lived in our house that wasn't ours, without a fireplace. K. was weighed on her feet from serving coffee in thick ceramic cups. I was coming home from a meditation group. Then my legs wouldn't work. I was made of flagstone, needing all sorts of tiny adjustments. Over our fireplace, cement glued differing continents together. Though I could hardly walk, a man living nearby asked me to sort through manuscripts, to count them. I started putting them into piles of ten. Their spines slid against each other. Shelley's *Queen Mab*, *The Descent of Alette*, a Collected Bishop, a rare Baldwin hidden under one stack, a melodrama of 2050. Now the man, now high & blotchy, ordered me to load his van. Bishop was one of the great mid-century poets, I instructed. He was on his way to the university at Davis, where he would rank writers. By the time I fitted towers of manuscripts in his van, some were re-congealing into their authors. This now bland man was abducting them, even put tape on their mouths after giving them drops of water that fell from their mouths. One escaped as I opened the back doors. He didn't see this. None must go free, he had said. I had to check the vents as he revved his engine. Tell me more about these prisoners, he asked. Was I still flagstone?

Between Species

This year a jellyfish dance party!
Streamers entangle.
No longer trapped in "personhood."
All enjoy invisible
synapses. We feel ourselves out,
& out as if parachutes.
Next year we will be "inanimate."
A horde of marble blue mushrooms
enter. Sea goats bifurcate under an aquamarine

disco ball. Sponges roam.
We float to the floor gladly,
& at the party's peak,
crawl on fungal highways.

Seaweed creates lineage,
& remember by breaking off—
to spread.

Demise of the Courier Pigeon

The Cincinnati Zoo left Martha
time to consider what the messages
in the sky meant.
Aging, she claw-clings her cage,
fathoms the miles, sensing some song
left on tiny scrolls.

Professor Whitman originally had six, &
bred Martha to mingle with rock doves,
trained them to be quicker, when her
vestal gaze told him: those two male birds,
        <well it wasn't happening>.

                At the zoo,
the rock doves cooed & died off, though
a prize called for a courier who could
mate Martha, yet she preferred
watching swallows manifest.

Her relatives were shot at, molested,
for carrying information:
the real aim was absolute flight.

Martha (c. 1885–September 1914) perched,
pert beak shut, for good,
feet frozen in a block of ice, now
        stuffed at the Smithsonian.

All the Men Disappear

from the family tree ledger—

—my mother's father visited once after the
Divorce: the small town quaked

at this Anna Maria, my grandmother, first to
have a typewriter & telephone.

He came one winter afternoon,
picked up my three-year-old mother &
spun her into crystal until he dissolved.

It's been this way, long years of a Spruce in lucid talks
with a Sempervirens. Anna Maria stares
into poppies & red ox-eye daisies.

We will cross that cataract later,
        a time-switch box opens, is
an insect dormitory with faded instructions.

Here, Major Oak small talks the mailbox.
Both use switch & time dialect
        that elixir us. Anxiety
tends to hide in the
        stored hurt that comes back:

*

 My mother eloped on the *Drottningholm*
sailing for New York—
For a decade after, Anna Maria sent letters on onionskin,
typescript or handwritten, ink drawings of trees, outsize houses,
flowers taller than her horses.
She mentions Beethoven, Hölderlin & Blavatsky &
American war bonds & offers scores for her accordion.
          Gold lights are on in her houses.
Memory loops like Dalarna flowers that stagger & spiral off pages.
A pale road from Falun goes across Fulufjället's mountain

*

The child left all her belongings in the road.

Lines dissolved into circles when it rained

so much the day he was interred.

Now she lay in her father's buried arms
          beneath her. The VA, falling apart with everything.
Those men have long gone, with father, —
          Plinths on the hills had to flatten.
Séances at the dining room were grandmother's idea . . .
Their breath is heavy, soft, at times wet.
I bring orchids, their ostentatious vascular
stems in a military green vase: they perform
          slow death, throw off tiny black powder specks . . .
How to grieve these men, busted
          by war, cocktail-clouded, & heart-heavy,
          the suits, the ties, the bars at family restaurants.

There are no measurable minerals from them that linger, they
      murmur before the gates shut before dark.

In winter visitors merge with sleepers in
      green-brown light:
remember to take all belongings
      before setting forth

Half Brother Lives on in Drafts

What did Chilly Lake say to Embers,
pretends to remember, prefers to forget.
Embers teach tiny spots to spread.
I don't burn, know early to
say sleepy. Freshly bathed,
dry my hair over the circling flame.
It jumps from stove to cotton gown
catches straw hair.
I wing like a whirlwind, to
half brother's door, shut like a firewall,
where *Hawaii Five-O* plays, ode to
his unmet dad born on the Big Island—
He is a prompt ghosty: rolls
me in flannel,
tumbles me out—
I had that glow of
being saved.
He races to tell our mother,
picketing five blocks away.
There's a tiny wiggle scar,
shaped like Norway's claw.
Heaving lake laugh.
Chilly remembers, he says
that he carried small cups of water
to save his stepfather
who drank, a cigarette falling while
he slept—Mother chose
to save him. Chilly howls when
seeing the gouged mattress
leaning against the trash bins.
I am Chilly's Houdini,
my thin wrists easily escape.

Brava, brava, Embers breathes—
Chilly would always love
fire trucks. Sirens
mesmerize, alcohol's quick tricks.
He took the stark, short sloping
road. Everyone has a
brother that is early starlight it seems.
He handed me a rose
in a dream   & helmed a court

Skull, with Your Teeth like Silver Armor

      Don't want to be dead
here on this perch, this art stand, so earthy.
Damien Hirst's skull thinks like this, this
studded death-head said to be worth 100 million,
part of an enormous hedge fund
billowing, while art triumphs
over kindness—like Hirst's shark shredding
(don't be late; show ends)—
for eyes hollowed out like this skull,
jewels painstakingly set & bordering
a nose smashed in, gaping teeth,
armor of open lost bright mouth.

When a viewer sees this skull, the viewer
has already tasted earth's dust,
not as much as a soldier who wears a skull.
He wore it like a stereophonic mask,
connected his iPod through a hollow
in his hooded sweatshirt.

This diamond-skull isn't memento mori,
it's a monument of, of
very inversion of art:
dead shark eye, jeweled, examines us.
"Skulls are in" a shopkeeper said,
stroking those of brandied caramel.

This soldier's skull has brain's imprint:
felt shark's luscious tongue, now
he is sewn, plaster-numb.
No decay for this hearse, hummer
of hummers flying dungeon streets—

Must we wear our death this way?
Trace of where brains
felt comfortably held,
out of the pan into apocalypse.

　　　　I wander like a zombie playing checkers
in my head, this soldier wore an iPod
dangling like an IV.
It's death's glucose drip, he says,
spindly curtains open
a window crack'd ajar,
saltwater whirled.

Decay is far away & ironic right
here in this museum, there's
flesh of saddest shark in all worlds,
Facebook of our times.
　　　　　　　This soldier danced
until he fell down dirty,
skull macerated to skin patched on
to wear a leopard's mask & him
clawing down into music along
veins in glucose drip.
This soldier fell from his brain.

　　　　SoHo is louder than usual with vanity
E-diamonds, the most durable, or
an invisible painting on auction;

soldier said dead thrice to prove he still lived
& wore a voodoo princess dress
& tin body parts nailed to his wood hut for cure.

Glucose could be thicker,
blood could be warmer. Skull had a
prayer rug under it
before Hirst's diamonds adhered.
They shone ice in aluminum buckets—
where tissue shrank away clean.

Artist not smartest harpoonist on earth
with grungy glass smile, won't wear
while soldier's consciousness
drags his bones behind.

Art, the man says, comes from some place
where nothing stares back; sipping his
bloody mary; dirty is as dirty does.
Tell this to skull, to stop shark shredding,
dying in public.

      This wasn't what soldier wanted skull
to remember. His buddy filmed it &
came back with everything in pieces.

Ovid During Lockdown

I breathe change into
        gods   vegetables insects   animals that

perfoliate in every air—I can rush, he says,
white blood cells on call. Cordyceps with caterpillar
fingers I am.

I asked to be a reed, a lily, an eel. I wanted to be
that forever autumn, flesh for germination.
A virus travels restlessly &
        chemistry inhabits & inhibits.
It takes one to live one—to taste disintegration.

        That woman's body looks like that Sycamore
with yellow flaking rashes. A tree in the distant
path is a human with its shifting molecules visible.

I can be the bride to
lymph lakes guarded by nymphs, yet they too
grow weary, spot another cloud out of a sky's sentence:
Cirrus crisis, then the Altostratus.—gaps between— .
                Air erases what germs it can.

Awareness flows. It must. Hurt color too.
Urgent Care closed.

A man wears a pizza box as a sun hat,
dragging trash entrails. Sycamore's rashes
drop like bark. Something will hatch.

I can grow a branch, or hoof, or
not take a drug for a drug-like effect.

Infection mutates, awaiting Apollo's heat cure:
the prickly pear—or—solar cashmere
enough to blaze several epidemics.

Infirmaries with seedlings born too soon . . .
Siri says she can't use past days.
I see a rippling dark canal then I am one.
I see my photo of a tree-tall sunflower. I can
be that face on a casual day, without coughing?

Dream Cure

In brightness, her horse she did acquit.
In zinc dress, her dress she did acquit.
Silver diva in haste, she mounted.
Her horse did speed through luminous
lush grass & pine.

Flourishing, she had known
her dress, too heavy,
it turned heads. She sped to edges
of city-forests, took high turns,
mountain narrows

to have the dream cure
—held above a volcanic world,
                              she

was both fed dreams & could
send them out, fast ticker tape.
She ate food that could not be known,
met those who can't be seen &

saw the heat vest one "soul" put on another,
or the cold chilling one. She sent
for a list of books, never came.
Her country had been taken.
Her bed frame stared & listened.

I ran toward her but we couldn't speak.
The beaded gown she did acquit.
A silver thing she fled, where hill
stopped horse, she stopped among
villagers. One even mixed

killing powders, herbal broths.

Her horse she set free, saw
racing hill & empty sky,
a way out she would of this *this*.
Fringed trees locked &
she couldn't remember the ship
or why she sent her horse away.

Millions lined up for deaths.

She saw someone she knew—
her own mother on unsteady ankles

in hospital gown.

She passed along with the crowd of
Mary blue & white gowns that kept falling
silly strings. They waited,
then taken where the dreams to be dreamed
flow down artichoke road.

Here were boat vest,
         horse stone & freshly cut branches.
She met Shakespeare rising from his crypt,
quickly tried following.

A single train leaves every day on time to carry
sadness building at a necessary rate
for speed until it finds some other track.
The boat vests had been tossed.
Rivers dried down.

Sometimes the heaviest get a chance
to go off course to a
small mountain dwelling.
Are you okay? Are you sure?
Days pass when no load passes.
Then light found the tunnel. Everything was

radiant in the best way.
My now dear small ones, I hold you.

Bright Unrest

after Jane Campion's Bright Star

1. He Was Dissolving in Her, Keats Said

Her guilt skirt of contracted pleats rustled heavily, of its
stitching I knew nothing. My Sibyl is comfortable
with her dyslexia

on the ground where energy flows upward into trees. There was
mushroom tulle, ruffling in her gown's counter-stitches
& ties across the midback.

In Jane Campion's film, even mourning is fashionable,
which sounds negative. I'm reconciled, given how much grief is
an art of trailing hawthorn cape.

If a woman can't speak her stitches, then what of her dress? Her
shorn tresses, jagged. Say something different. To be of
the heath now.

The sticking poverty, even with such dress, especially the subtle bubbling up
threads of her who haunts him filamentally, I mean that as

stubble too. Her too.
O Fanny. Heath black bramble grief-art of cross-stretch stuck in
the goss:
he was dissolving in her, & said, at lastly, was it dream or sleep?

Sybil feels strange like the mark for reversal
in editor's marks. He lay on top of the lime bower in reversal,
& fetal, each to each, they curled into—

—both tuning forks for energy, first-fresh.
Circle around the stitchwork; English oak coming out.
The poem is invisible too, can I say?

[my student complained because the film wasn't from Keats's point
of view but wasn't that the point; I liked him
before he said that, and then still, but why had he said that]

Then the man who loved Keats more than Fanny (so he thought) &
could get one with child only who'd been a practical stranger except
for her scones. She was her art of scones like swans & alone; he
that never charmed Fanny struck back, and abandoned—still

I listen
          —cloud berries growing in a butterfly farm helps
though the carcasses are swept up with a

stiff broom, hair strands like S's, aged leaves of
summer, turned muff-gray.
She stood in the alien corn; dead star-eye gives no relief.

Breath, a jealousy guarding always that
intelligence of webs.
Phylactery of twine,

space where all that dissolves joins?

II. On Seeing Jane Campion at a Second Screening of *Bright Star*

At the Aero Theatre Abbie Cornish was there not as plump and young
Campion is now rereading Motion's biography of Keats
   "Mr. Brown" is not as bad but still he hates himself
Making the film was like a dream
The cinematographer kept the camera & equipment as far
from the people and children as he could "Inside"
time protracted so
the room was full of butterflies needing very warm temperature

III. After Reading Andrew Motion's Biography of Keats

Nightingales swarmed the heath when I walked there
(poor Tom is still on welk walk)
At Hampstead let me be shakespeared to many selves
When I walked the river's edge
London petered out in primrose & sedge
Everyone pressed so upon me in any room
Claret rises to apartments in my brain unknown,
I'm filament charged against my time
& Byron at my narrow coffin desk in mad pursuit
in this "soul-making vale,"

       against chameleon time
           I have always writ in unrest

The Clairvoyant Heart

I knew a young man who carried
cheer wherever he traveled.
I knew him for his delivery
of manuscripts, his special key,
his motorcycle, & peculiar zest.
Glad, he walked among us. I
even told him "I love you."

No one wanted him to leave,
but he went on a trip, sent back
a montage of daredevil
play, like jumping into the seat
of a moving car, laughing,
swinging his arms. He went home

to die. He had cancer (none of us knew).
Walking an icicled path,
he heard the contrapuntal
dialogue between ravens & doves.
He was so light & airy, his heart,

not in denial, just slipping, ever so
slowly, into suspenseful bliss.

Leaving the Ice Hotel

Every drop was measured by one
child eye that was millions, folding the four-cornered
frostbitten blanket, packed for
all exigencies,
& so many expedition cars to burn:
what happens to the lily
happens to everyone.

Pack your sweat-clothes before
whiteouts, sky rivers
in sudden whiplash
from summered winter . . .
Ghosts on bench after bench,
hats only visible above shaken molecules.

Catch a numbing walk before you leave
for the ice hotel. Try not to hear of
the whale with injured spine breaststroking
more than three thousand miles.

All close against heat;
& canyons quit.
Mouths agape at a perpetual what next;
infants sleep in the slight, sturdy place
hidden under the table, built with
discarded weak timber—;

December in April spits hail.

Here, at home, neighbors live in barracks,
with yachts. One parks out front, soon to rendezvous
with other vehicles, all autonomous! Debris
drapes wires, poles, edifices.
No freedom in the mountains.
There's unprecedented powder, then none at all.
Never like this, you say; no, never.

I pined for the ice hotel.
It was my church,
necessarily unknowable.
Then reading of accidents on thin ice,
landslides & more

—I regret
our conscious & unconscious footprints
that won't faint away.
Flashbacks of crisp visits, I bluster in,
deplaning a sky train,
surrounded by warm fog.
On the deck, my
mufflers useless, as is my all-weather
expansive coat—
I strain
to glimpse frozen immovables.
Once ambling ice had freewill. Now
in conservatory empty lifts.

Where were our heights—ceilings with
unbreakable intention, glitter shroud,
& those solid blue blocks as beds
here last century, or so?

Summer had no gleaming harvest.
Not enough ice to sculpt
couches, closets for pelts, parkas;
not enough frames, beds for
phones, car parks.

Anyhow I arrive, gates bolted—
. . . it is bright,
stark with cold-dust, a
firecracker broth for supping
                    at the raining pagoda.

I wear a
degraded fire-suit,
my spruce with one continuous eye on
lake horizons, the other eye tracking
wild hedges—nothing
pretending to last.

Breathing the Weather

The hail of summer, tender of snow.
   A child hears meltdowns thumping in
her chest, choking when
   she reaches into gruff bark.

Oxygen of chase, soot of youth,
remember of teeth, forget of giving up.

l learn of the goose who with her beak
parts milk from water. lt
is sure of itself.

I'm on a bench,
   shivering, forming flecks
     from this week's seasons, bamboo
stalks everywhere:

   summer mixed into the salad of a winter weeklong of
quick living, night rain, unstopping but stop
it would.
Strawberries wince,
     grapes worry,
    as do fluffy black bees & the complete aerial realm;
can we please the bird and fish?

Medicate of lupine, heal of soapberry.
Wise of elderberries, trail of electric
rattling, binding
   heal of laughter, caffein-ate of clarity,

folded, stiff handkerchief of the Sierras,
& there's never before seen

Alps of the Hollywood sign—

while unseen geese try to keep distinctions.

Notes

"I Take Off the Suit of Never Mind" is in part inspired by "Luriana, Lurilee," a garden poem written by Charles Isaac Elton (1839-1900), quoted by Virginia Woolf in *To the Lighthouse*.

"Tjikko" is located in Fulufjället National Park of Dalarna, Sweden. It is said to be 9,550 years old. For millennia, the tree appeared in a stunted shrub formation due to the harsh extremes in which it lives. During the warming of the twentieth century, the tree sprouted into a normal tree formation. The husband and wife who discovered the tree, scientists Leif Kullman and Lisa Öberg, gave the tree its nickname, "Old Tjikko," after their dog.

"On Coffee in Canada" borrows a line from Rufus Wainwright's "Cigarettes and Chocolate Milk": "those other things which for several reasons we won't mention."

"Apparitional," by way of dream, is written in memoriam of poet 'Annah Sobelman.

"Between Species" was inspired in part by *In the Deep I* and *II* (thread and ink on canvas) by Karen Simon.

Acknowledgments

Poems in this volume have appeared elsewhere: "Ovid During Lockdown," *The Last Milkweed* anthology (Tupelo Press, 2024); "Tasting the Last of the Ice Age," *Poem-a-Day*, Academy of American Poets; "Lake at the End Of," "When in Love Goes Fear," and "Bright Unrest," *Lana Turner*; "Dream Cure" (as "Godiva's Dream Cure"), *Taos Journal of Poetry*; "Skull, with Your Teeth like Silver Armor" (as "Or Wend, Skull with Your Teeth like Bright Armor"), Winning Writers War Poetry Contest 2009, third prize; "Dead I've Spoken to Lately" and "On Coffee in Canada En Route to (and from) Elizabeth Bishop's Childhood Home," *Bombay Gin*.

First, let me thank my fantastic editor, Stephanie G'Schwind, at The Center for Literary Publishing at Colorado State University. I appreciate all the editorial staff who worked so rigorously on this book.

Gratitudes go to an inspiring presence, reader, writer, translator par excellence, Catherine Theis (and her dear ones, Lou and Aaron).

Thank you, Brenda Hillman, for your friendship and for being a beacon for what it means to be a citizen and poet. Thank you, Marilyn McCabe Seeman, for always believing in my poetry, and almost lifelong friend Brian Lizotte, for your painting and inspirational comments on my writing. Thank you, Laura Baker, for your instructions on "the lake pose" (viparita karani)—offering a meditative state that aided the process of writing. Thank you, Gayle Stuart Fiedler-Vierma: your good humor has meant the world to me—we met during Covid on Zoom Iyengar practice. Heaps of thanks to you, Nancy Sandercock: your extraordinary teaching delights and supports me. There is no one like you.

Special thanks for inspirations from those in my stratosphere for their art-of-living and writing: Diana Arterian, Cal Bedient, Molly Bendall, Janalynn Bliss, Amaranth Borsuk, Anna Fyta, Alexandria Hall, Cynthia Hogue, Forrest Gander, Pamela Gray, David St. John, Dana Johnson, Liz Johnson, Anna

Journey, Shirin and Maja Lillijeqvist, Erin Lynch, Doug Manuel, Steven Aaron Minas, Sawnie Morris, Michelle Orsi, the late great Marjorie Perloff, Catherine Pond, Donald Revell, Thomas Renjilian, Austen Leah Rosenfeld, Judith and David Sensibar, Suzanne Simard, Karen Simon, Callie Siskel, Lindsey Skillen, Demetres Tryphonopoulos, Stephen Yenser, and eco-activist artist Wendy Welch.

I owe my life to the poets of the past—and to the "Mother Trees" and all the forests we depend upon, without which, we are in complete hell.

As always, I am grateful to my darling Kate Marie Chandler, for everything.

This book is set in Calluna & Twentieth Century
by The Center for Literary Publishing
at Colorado State University.

Copyediting by Erin Peters.
Proofreading by Maia Coen.
Book design & typesetting by Natalia Sperry.
Cover art by Karen Simon.
Cover design by Chase Cate.
Printing by Books International.